The bells; drama in three acts - Primary Source Edition

Leopold Lewis

THE BELLS

DRAMA
IN THREE ACTS

BY

LEOPOLD LEWIS

Adapted for performance by Male Characters, and supplied
with full directions for stage management,
diagrams, etc.

BY

C. J. BIRBECK

Professor of Elocution and English Literature

NEW YORK

JOSEPH F. WAGNER

Copyright, 1904, by JOSEPH F. WAGNER, New York

THE BELLS.

ARGUMENT.

This play was founded on "The Polish Jew," a dramatic study of M. M. Erckmann—Chatrian.

Mathias, who forms a central figure through the entire play, had been, at a period of some fifteen years prior to opening of the first act, in very distressing circumstances; in fact poverty and ruin stared him in the face. He owed a sum of money which he was unable to pay.

One stormy night, the snow falling heavily, there came to the inn of which he was the keeper, a traveller who bore the appearance and in reality was, a Polish Jew. Whilst his horse and sleigh were being cared for by the hostler, he warmed himself by the fire and partook of some refreshments. At the expiration of about an hour he prepared for his departure. He took some money from a girdle which he wore about his waist and in doing so displayed a great quantity of golden coin.

Mathias, though previously a comparatively honest man, was sorely tempted. He saw an opportunity of retrieving his lost fortunes and, heedless of his conscience which smote him terribly, he determined to kill the Jew and possess himself of his gold.

He concealed himself some distance from the inn and when the Jew had seen his horse harnessed to the sleigh and had proceeded some way on his journey, Mathias, disguised, rushed from an ambush, axe in hand and followed closely after the sleigh.

He struck and killed the Jew, wrenched the girdle containing the money from the body, and in order to conceal the manner of the murder, he threw the corpse into his own lime kiln where it was consumed. He was never suspected.

The nervous dread proceeding from the remorse which Mathias now feels, the frequent hallucinations, the jingling of sleigh bells, which he imagines he hears, terrorize him and fill his family and guests with wonder and dismay.

CHARACTERS OF THE PLAY.

MATHIAS. The Burgomaster.
CHRISTIAN. A young Officer.
WILHELM. Brother to Mathias.
HANS,
FATHER WALTER, } Farmers.
PRESIDENT of the Court.
CLERK of the Court.
A MESMERIST.
A NOTARY.
DOCTOR ZIMMER.
FRANZ. A servant to Mathias.
TONY,
KARL, } Guests.
FRITZ,
POLISH JEW.
Judges, Barristers, Gendarmes, Guests, The Public.

COSTUMES.

MATHIAS. Black coat, high yellow vest, black knee-breeches, black cloth leggings—large fur coat and fur cap.

2nd dress. Drab coat and knee-breeches—stockings and buckled shoes. Iron-gray wig—smooth face—heavy eyebrows.

3rd dress. Blouse with hood.

CHRISTIAN. Officer's hussar uniform, boots and spurs. Blond wig and moustache.

HANS,
WALTER, } Similar to Mathias' dress. Gray wigs.
WILHELM,

FRANZ. Brown velveteen knee-breeches, gray stockings, shoes—white ballet shirt—red vest—waiter's apron. Black short-curled wig.

MESMERIST. Clothes entirely black—white turnover collar—long black hair—black moustache and chin beard—very pale makeup—eyes made very prominent.

NOTARY. Black coat, vest, breeches, stockings. Buckled shoes. Ruffled front to shirt. White dress wig. Makeup old.

PRESIDENT,
JUDGES, } Black gowns—caps—white bag wigs.

BARRISTERS,
CLERK, } ditto.

DR. ZIMMER. Dressed like the Notary. Gray wig.

POLISH JEW. Large cloak—fur cap—dark underclothes. Black wig and beard.

THE GUESTS. Like Mathias' second dress. Makeup youthful.

PROPERTIES.

Act I.

White snow cloth down on stage from the 3rd up to 5th entrance, inclusive. Table and 3 chairs R. and L. Stove, kettle, etc., R. Sideboard L. Spinning wheel and stool center. Large clock, hands to work, up L. Several chairs and an oaken settee. Glasses, decanters and fancy china on sideboard. Several lighted candles on table R. Gun and game bag for Hans. Bottle of wine and glass for Franz, off L. 2 E. Lantern to be lighted for Franz. Wind outside. Snow falling all through act. Jug of wine for Franz. Glass to break in prompt entrance. Jewel box for Mathias, containing a necklace. Tray containing supper, wine, napkins, etc. Sleigh bells in prompt entrance. Curtain on window.

Act II.

Carpet down. Fire in grate up center—tongs. Cabinet up L. Sofa down R. Table and 3 armchairs L. Chairs about the room. Desk down L. to be locked—key. Pens, ink and paper on table. Church bells outside. Snuff box for Mathias. Bunch of keys for Mathias. Large leather bag of (coin) money in desk. Book for Franz. Portfolio and sealed documents for Notary.

Act III.

(*In court room.*)

Carpet down. Judge's desk center. Table R. and L.—chairs. Armchair R. center for Mathias. Papers and documents on tables and desk. Guns for Gendarmes.

(In bedroom). Chintz curtains on alcove L. Table at alcove, also chair. Bed in alcove, chairs R. Lighted candle on table. Bottle of water and glass for Franz. Key in door R. Sleigh bells in prompt entrance. Chime of church bells off stage.

ABBREVIATED STAGE DIRECTIONS.

The actor is supposed to be facing the audience.

L.	Right of stage.	L.	Left of stage.
L. I. E.—Right first entrance.		L. I. E.—Left first entrance.	
L. 2 E.—Right sec'd entrance.		L. 2 E.—Left second entrance.	
etc.		etc.	
L. U. E.—Right upper entrance.		L. U. E.—Left upper entrance.	
D. R. F.—Door in right flat.		D. L. F.—Door in left flat.	

Flat, means the scene running across the back of the stage.

R. C.—Right center of stage. L. C.—Left center of stage.

R. Cor.—Right corner. L. Cor.—Left corner.

C. D.—Center door.

C.—Center of stage.

Up.—Up stage toward the rear.

Down.—Down stage toward the audience.

X.—To cross the stage.

X's R.—To cross to the right of stage.

X's L.—To cross to the left of stage.

A Drop.—A scene let down from above.

Time of Representation.—One hour and three-quarters.

Place of Action.—Alsace.

Period.—The winter of 1833.

SCENERY.

ACT I.

Village Inn.   *Double Set.*

: *Snowy Landscape drop in 5 showing bridge.*

R.5.E   *Snow covered wings*   Burning Lime Kiln.   *Snow covered wings*   L.S.E.

R.4.E.   L.4.E

Gauze drop

Kitchen drop in 3.

Chair   *Large window*   Chair   Door   Large Cloch

Door   Sideboard

                    Spinning   Stool   Door
                    wheel

        Chair   Stove

        Chair   Table   Chair   Chair   Table   Chair

R I.E.   L.I.E.

Act II.

Parlor in the Burgomaster's House.

Street drop in 5 showing snow covered buildings.

Plain Chamber boxed in 4

Act III.

Double Set.

Front Set—Burgomaster's bedchamber.

Back Set—Courtroom interior.

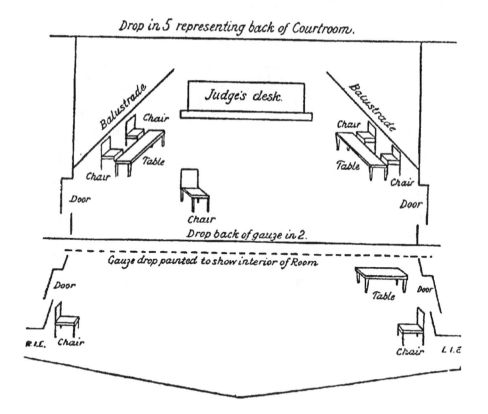

Drop in 5 representing back of Courtroom.

THE BELLS.

ACT I.

*Interior of a Village Inn in Alsace. A kitchen drop in 3, having a large window R. and door L. (in drop). Snowy landscape backing. Sides boxed to 1st entrance R. and L. Door R. 3 E. Door L. 2 E. Stove at R. 2 E.—kettle on stove. Sideboard with china and glasses near L. 1 2. Table down R.—3 chairs at table. Several other chairs—oak settee. Lamp burning on table R. Table L. chair. Spinning wheel and stool up center. Large clock, hands to work up in L. corner. It is Christmas Eve. Snow falling outside, which must be seen through window and when door opens. *Music at rise. Lights up, but the border lights back of 3 to be dim. Wind and sleigh bells to work in prompt entrance.*

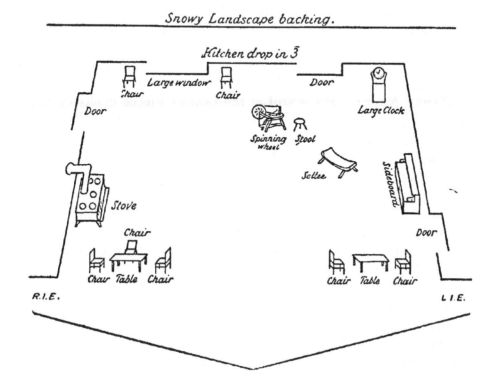

WILHELM. (*disc. at stove* R.) HANS *passes window; enters through door at back; he is covered with snow; he carries a gun, and a large game bag is slung across his shoulders.*

HANS. (*taking off his hat and shaking away the snow*) More snow, Master Wilhelm, more snow! (*He places his gun by the side of the stove.*)

WILHELM. Still in the village, Hans?

HANS. Yes, on Christmas eve one may be forgiven some small indulgence.

WILHELM. You know your sack of flour is ready for you at the mill?

HANS. Oh, yes; but I am not in a hurry. Father Walter will take charge of it for me in his cart. Now one glass of wine, and then I'm off. (*he sits at table,* R., *laughing*)

WILHELM. Father Walter still here? I thought he had left long ago.

HANS. No. no. He is still at the Golden Fleece emptying his bottle. As I came along, I saw his cart standing outside the grocer's, with the coffee, the cinnamon, and the sugar, all covered with snow, he, he, he! He is a jolly old fellow. Fond of good wine, and I don't blame him, you may be sure. We shall leave together.

WILHELM. And you have no fear of being upset?

HANS. What does it matter? As I said before, on Christmas eve one may be forgiven some small indulgence.

WILHELM. I will lend you a lantern when you go. (*calling*) Franz! Franz!

FRANZ. (*off* L.) Yes, sir!

WILHELM. Some wine for Hans!

FRANZ. Yes, sir.

HANS. That's the sort. Considering the festive character of weather like this, one really must take something.

WILHELM. Yes, but take care, our white wine is very strong.

HANS. Oh, never fear. But, where is our Burgomaster? Iow is it he is not to be seen? Is he ill?

WILHELM. No, my brother, the Burgomaster went to Ribeau-ille five days ago.

(*Enter* FRANZ *from door* L. 2 E., *crosses over table* R. *and places decanter of white wine and glasses upon it.*)

FRANZ. Here is the wine Master Hans.

(*Exit* FRANZ *door* L.)

HANS. Good, good! (*he pours out a glass, and drinks with gusto*) I wager, now, that the Burgomaster has gone to buy the vine for the wedding.

WILHELM. (*laughing*) Not at all improbable.

HANS. Only, just now, when I was at the Golden Fleece, it vas talked about publicly, that the pretty Annette, the daughter of he Burgomaster, and Christian, the Quartermaster of Gen-larmes, were going to be married! I could scarcely believe my :ars. Christian is certainly a brave man, and an honest man, and ι handsome man! I do not wish to maintain anything to the :ontrary. Our village is rather distinguished in that respect. (*pulls up his shirt collar*) But he has nothing but his pay to live ιpon, whilst Annette is the richest match in the village.

WILHELM. Do you believe then, Hans, that money ought ιlways to be the one consideration?

HANS. No, no, certainly not—on the contrary. Only, I thought that the Burgomaster——

WILHELM. Well, you have been mistaken; Mathias did not even ask, "What have you?" He said at once, "Let Annette give her free consent, and I give mine!"

HANS. And did she give her free consent?

WILHELM. Yes; she loves Christian, and as my brother has no thought but the happiness of his child, he does not look for wealth.

HANS. Oh, if the Burgomaster consents and you consent, and Annette consents, why, I suppose I cannot refuse my consent either. Only, I may make this observation, I think Christian a very lucky dog, and I wish I was in his place!

(FATHER WALTER *passes the window and enters; he is covered with snow which he brushes off; he then goes down* R. *to the back of table.*)

WALTER. Ha! Ha! There you are, Hans, taking care that the inner man will not suffer on this stormy Christmas eve. Good evening, Master Wilhelm! How is the lovely Annette whom they say Christian is about to carry off?

HANS. What an old fool you are, Walter!

(*Enter* FRANZ *through door* L. *and places a lighted lantern on the sideboard* L., *he exits.*)

WALTER. Well, I am afraid there is a pair of us; but what is the meaning of that lantern?

HANS. Why, to act as a light for the cart.

WILHELM. (*goes to sideboard and blows out the light in the lantern*) Now, you can go by moonlight.

WALTER. Yes, yes; certainly we will go by the light of the moon. Let us empty a glass in honor of the young couple. (*they fill glasses*) Here's to the health of Christian and Annette!

(*they drink—*HANS *taking a long time in drinking the contents of his glass, and then heaving a deep sigh, and Music commences.*)

WALTER. (*seriously*) And now listen; as I entered I saw Christian returning with two gendarmes, and I am sure that in a quarter of an hour——

WILHELM. (*goes up to window*) Listen! The wind is rising (*wind off stage quite loud*) I hope Mathias is not now on the road. Ah! it is Christian! (**music forte*) (CHRISTIAN *passes the window and enters door; he is covered with snow.*)

OMNES. Christian! (*music stops*)

CHRIS. Good evening all. (*He takes off his hat and lays it on table* L.; *he brushes the snow from his clothing and sits at* R. *of table* L.)

WILHELM. Where have you come from, Christian?

CHRIS. From the Hóvald! From the Hóvald! What, a snow-storm! I have seen many in Auvergne or the Pyrenees, but never anything like this. (WILHELM *goes off* L. *door and returns with a jug of wine which he places on the stove—Takes a glass from the sideboard and places it on table* L.) I have been five hours on duty in the snow, on the Hóvald.

WILHELM. You have been five hours in the snow, Christian! Your duties must be terribly severe.

CHRIS. How can it be helped? At two o'clock we received information that smugglers had passed the river the previous night, with tobacco and gunpowder; so we were bound to be off at once.

WILHELM. (*pours hot wine from jug into glass and hands it to* CHRISTIAN) Drink this Christian, it will warm you.

CHRIS. Thank you, Wilhelm (*drinks*) Ah! that's good.

WALTER. The Quartermaster is not difficult to please. (**Music.*)

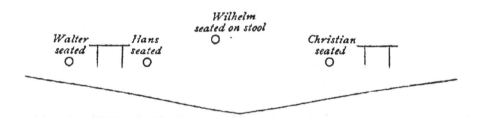

WILHELM. (*to* CHRISTIAN) Never mind, Christian, you are fortunate to have arrived thus early! (*wind heard off*) Listen to the wind! I hope that Mathias will have the prudence to stop for shelter somewhere on the road.

CHRIS. Your winters are very severe here.

WALTER. Oh, not every year, Quartermaster! For fifteen years we have not had a winter so severe as this.

HANS. No—I do not remember to have seen so much snow since what is called "The Polish Jew's Winter." In that year the Schnieberg was covered in the first days of November, and the frost lasted till the end of March.

CHRISTIAN. And for that reason it is called "The Polish Jew's Winter?"

WALTER. No—It is for another and terrible reason, which none of us will ever forget. Master Wilhelm remembers it well, I am sure.

WILHELM. You are right, Walter, you are right.

HANS. Had you been here at that time, Quartermaster, you might have won your cross.

CHRIS. How?

(HANS *and* WALTER *smoking*—CHRISTIAN *occasionally drinking his wine.*)

WALTER. I can tell you all about this affair from the beginning to the end, since I saw it nearly all myself. Curiously enough, it was this very day, just fifteen years ago, that I was seated at this very table. There was Mathias, who sat there, and who had only bought his mill just six months before; there was old John Roebec, who sat there—they used to call him "the Little Shoe-maker;" and several others, who are now sleeping under the turf—we shall all go there some day! Happy are those who have nothing upon their conscience! We were just beginning a game of cards, when, just as the old clock struck ten, the sound of horse bells was heard; a sledge stopped before the door, and almost immediately afterwards a Polish Jew entered. He was a well-made, vigorous man, between forty and fifty years of age. I fancy I can see him even now entering at that door with his green cloak and his fur cap, his large black beard and his great boots covered with hare skin. He was a seed merchant. He said as he came in, "Peace be with you!" Everybody turned to look at him, and thought, "Where has he come from? What does he want?" Because you must know that the Polish Jews who come to dispose of seed do not arrive in this province till the month of February. Mathias said to him, "What can I do for you?" But the Jew, without replying, first opened his cloak, and then unbuckled a girdle which he wore round his waist. This he threw upon the table, and we all heard the ringing sound of the gold it contained! Then he said, "The snow is deep; the road difficult; put my horse in the stable. In one hour I shall continue my journey." After that he drank his wine without speaking to any one, and sat like a man depressed, and who is anxious about his affairs. At eleven o'clock the Night Watchman came in. Every one went his way, and the Jew was left alone!

(*Chord of Music—loud gust of wind—crash of glass off at* L.
*—hurry—*ALL *start to their feet—Music continued*)

WILHELM. What has happened? I must go and see—I will
return immediately. (*exits door* L.)

(*The others resume their seats.*)

CHRIS. But I do not yet see how I could have gained the
cross in this affair——

WALTER. Stop a minute. The next morning they found the
Jew's horse dead under the Bridge of Vechem, and a hundred
yards further on, the green cloak and the fur cap, deeply stained
with blood. As to what became of the Jew himself has never to
this day been discovered. (*Music ceases*)

HANS. Everything that Walter has stated is strictly true.
The gendarmes came here the next morning, notwithstanding
the snow; and, in fact, it is since that dreadful time that the
brigade has been established here.

CHRIS. But was no inquiry instituted?

HANS. Inquiry! I should think there was. It was the former
Quartermaster, Kelz, who undertook the case. How he travelled
about! What witnesses he badgered! What clues he discovered!
What information and reports were written! and how the coat
and the cap were analysed, and examined by magistrates and
doctors!—but it all came to nothing!

CHRIS. But, surely, suspicion fell on someone.

HANS. Oh, of course, the gendarmes are never at a loss for
suspicions in such cases. But proofs are required. About that
time, you see, there were two brothers living in the village who
had an old bear, with his ears all torn, two big dogs, and a
donkey, that they took about with them to the fairs, and made
the dogs bait the bear. This brought them a great deal of money;
and they lived a rollicking dissipated life. When the Jew disappeared, they happened to be at Vechem; suspicions fastened upon
them, and the report was, that they had caused the Jew to be
eaten by the dogs and the bear, and that they only refrained from
swallowing the cloak and cap, because they had had enough.
They were arrested, and it would have gone hard with the poor
devils, but Mathias interested himself in their case, and they
were discharged, after being in prison fifteen months. That was
the specimen of suspicion of the case.

CHRIS. What you have told me greatly astonishes me. I never heard a word of this before.

(*Re-enters* WILHELM *door* L.; *he crosses behind table and then goes to center.*)

WILHELM. Confound that fellow Franz! I was sure he left the windows in the kitchen open, and now every pane of glass in them is broken. I must tell you Christian that Fritz is outside. He wishes to speak with you.

CHRIS. Fritz the gendarme?

WILHELM. Yes, I asked him to come in, but he would not. It is upon some matter of duty.

CHRIS. Ah! good, I know what it is! (*he rises, takes up his hat and goes to door in drop*)

WILHELM. You will return, Christian?

CHRIS. In a few minutes. (*exits*)

WALTER. Ah! there goes a brave young fellow—gentle in character, I will admit, but not a man to trifle with rogues.

HANS. Yes, Mathias is fortunate in finding so good a son-in-law; but everything has succeeded with Mathias for the last fifteen years. (*Music commences*) He was comparatively poor then, and now he is one of the richest men in the village, and the Burgomaster. He was born under a lucky star.

WALTER. Well, and he deserves all the success he has achieved.

WILHELM. Hark! (x's *up to* L. *of door*)

HANS. It is, perhaps, Christian returning as he promised.

(*Music becomes stronger.*)

(MATHIAS *passes the window, then enters at* C. *door; he wears a long cloak covered with snow, large cap made of otter's skin, gaiters and spurs, and carries a large riding whip in his hand—tableau.*)

MATH. It is I—It is I! (*Music ceases*)

WILHELM. Mathias! Brother.

WALTER. }
HANS.   } (*starting up*) The Burgomaster!

WILHELM. You have come at last.

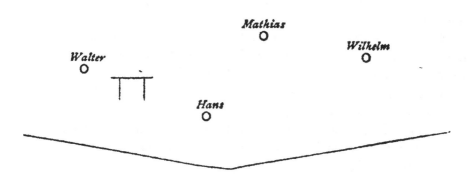

MATH. Yes, yes! Heaven be praised! What a snow storm.
vas obliged to leave the carriage at Vechem. It will be brought
er to-morrow.

WILHELM. (*taking his coat*) Let me take this off for you. I
ı very glad you did not stop away. We were becoming very
xious about you.

MATH. So I thought, Wilhelm; and that is the reason I
termined to reach home to-night. (*he looks around and goes
er to table* R.; *he takes off his hat and gives it to* WILHELM)
ı! ha! Father Walter and Hans you will have nice weather in
ıich to go home. (*to* WILHELM) Brother, tell Franz to have
ese things dried. (MATHIAS *sits* L. *of table* R.)

WILHELM. (*goes to door* L *and calls*) Franz! Franz, you lazy
scal, get your master's supper ready at once, and tell Nickel to
ke the horse to the stable. (HANS *and* WALTER *sit at table* R.)

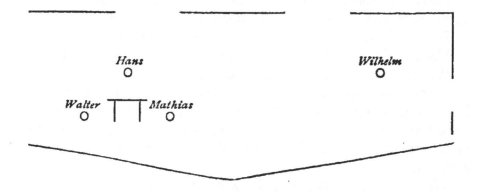

FRANZ. (*within*) Yes, sir; yes, sir; I will.

WILHELM. We thought perhaps that your cousin Bôth would have detained you.

MATH. (*unbuttoning his gaiters*) Oh, I had finished all my business yesterday morning, and I wished to come away; but Bôth made me stop to see a performance in the town.

WILHELM. A performance! Is Punchinello at Ribeauville? (WILHELM *goes to* L. C., *down stage.*)

MATH. No, it was not Punchinello. It was a Parisian who did extraordinary tricks. He sent people to sleep.

WILHELM. Sent people to sleep!

MATH. Yes.

WILHELM. He gave them something to drink, no doubt.

MATH. No; he simply looked at them and made signs, and they went fast asleep.—It certainly was an astonishing performance. If I had not myself seen it I should never have believed it.

HANS. Ah! the Brigadier Stenger was telling me about it the other day. He had seen the same thing at Saverne. This Parisian sends people to sleep, and when they are asleep he makes them tell him everything that weighs upon their consciences.

MATH. Everything—Wilhelm?

WILHELM. Yes, brother.

MATH. Look in the big pocket of my cloak. (*Enter* FRANZ *from* L. 2 *door—he goes to center*) Here Franz take these gaiters and spurs; hang them in the stable with the harness.

FRANZ. Yes, Burgomaster. (*exit* FRANZ *through door in drop*)

WILHELM. (*coming down stage with box*) What is it, Mathias?

MATH. (*rising*) Open the box. (WILHELM *opens box—the others approach and look at it—shows a handsome necklace.*)

HANS. How very handsome! Is it for Annette?

MATH. For whom else should it be? Not for Franz, I fancy.

WALTER. Ha! ha! what will Christian say?

MATH. He will say she is the prettiest girl in the Province. It is my wedding present for Annette. On the day of her marriage I wish her to wear it, and to preserve it forever. In fifteen or twenty years hence I hope she will remember her father gave it to her.

WILHELM. I warrant you she will never forget it.

MATH. All I wish is to see her happy with Christian. And
ow for supper and some wine. (*to* WALTER *and* HANS) You
ill stop and take a glass of wine with me?

WALTER. With pleasure, Burgomaster. (*all sit at table* R.)

HANS. For you, Burgomaster, we will try and make a
ittle effort.

(*Enter* FRANZ, *door* L. *with tray of supper and wine which he
places on table* R.; MATHIAS *helps the others to wine, and
begins to eat with good appetite.* FRANZ *closes the curtains
on window and exits door* L. 2 E.)

MATH. There is one advantage about the cold. It gives you
good appetite. Here's to your health! (*he drinks*)

WALTER.
HANS. } Here's yours, Burgomaster!

(*they touch glasses
and drink*)

MATH. Christian has not been here this evening?

WILHELM. Yes; they came to fetch him, but he will return
resently.

MATH. Ah! Good! good!

WILHELM. He came late to-day, in consequence of some duty
e had to perform in the Hôvald, in the capture of smugglers.

MATH. (*eating*) Nice weather for such a business. By the
ide of the river, I found the snow five feet deep.

WALTER. Yes; we were talking about that. We were telling
he Quartermaster, that since the "Polish Jew's Winter" we had
ever seen weather like this.

(MATHIAS *who was raising the glass to his lips—places it on
the table again without drinking.*)

MATH. Ah! you were talking of that!

(*distant sound of Bells heard—to himself—*"Bells! Bells!"
*—his whole aspect changes, and he leaves off eating, and
sits listening—the Bells continue louder*)

HANS. That winter, you remember, Burgomaster, the whole
valley was covered several feet deep with snow, and it was a long
time before the horse of the Polish Jew could be dug out.

MATH. (*with assumed indifference*) Very possibly; but that
tale is too old! It is like an old woman's story now, and is
thought about no more. (*watching them and starting up*) Do
you not hear the sound of Bells upon the road? (*the Bells still
go on*)

HANS. 〉 (*listening*) Bells? No!
WALTER. 〉

WILHELM. What is the matter, brother? You appear to be
ill. I will go and get you some hot wine.   (*exits door* L. 2 E.)

MATH. Thank you; it is nothing.

WALTER. Come, Hans, let us go and see to the horse. At the
same time, it is very strange that it was never discovered who
did the deed.

MATH. The rogues have escaped, more's the pity. Here's
your health! (*Music*)

WALTER. 〉 Thank you!
HANS. 〉

HANS. It is just upon the stroke of ten! (*they drink, and go
out together at door in drop* L.)

MATH. (*alone—comes forward and listens with terror—
Music with frequent chords) Bells! Bells! (*he runs to the
window and slightly drawing the curtains, looks out*) No one on
the road. (*comes forward*) What is this jingling in my ears?
What is to-night? Ah, it is the very night—the very hour! (*clock
strikes ten*) I feel a darkness coming over me. (*stage darkens*)
A sensation of giddiness seizes me. (*he staggers to chair*) Shall
I call for help? No, no, Mathias. Have courage! The Jew is
dead!

(*He sinks on chair* L. *of* R. *table. The Bells are louder—
stage and house dark. The back drop goes up and the stage
calcium lights are thrown on the scene, set behind. This
is shown to the audience through a gauze drop. The scene
is a snow-covered landscape and bridge drop in* 5. *Snow*

wings—snow cloth down on stage and snow falling. Lime-
kiln burning up left. Bells sound nearer and nearer. A
horse and sleigh—a man in the sleigh, enter L. 4 E. *Attached to*
the runners of the sleigh are wheels to facilitate easy move-
ment. They cross up to R. 5 E. *A man in cap and blouse*
carrying an axe follows in the snow—the axe is uplifted.
Bells stop. *Music tremulo continues.)

MATH. (*his back to scene*) Oh, it is nothing. It is the wine
and cold that have overcome me!

(*he rises and turns, goes up stage; starts violently upon seeing*
the vision before him; at the same time the JEW *in the*
sledge suddenly turns his face, which is ashy pale, and fixes
his eyes sternly upon him; MATHIAS *utters a prolonged*
cry of terror, and falls senseless—hurried Music)

QUICK CURTAIN.

END OF THE FIRST ACT.

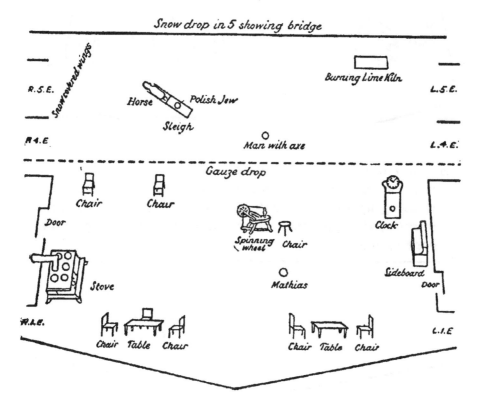

ACT II.

*Parlor in the Burgomaster's house. Plain chamber boxed in 4.
Two windows R. and L. in flat, fireplace and grate between them.
Door R. and L. Carpet down. Sofa right—table and armchairs L. Cabinet up in L. corner. Desk down near L. I. E.
Chairs about the rooms. Time, morning. Lights up full. *Music
at rise of curtain. Fire in grate—tongs. Pens, ink and paper on
the table.*

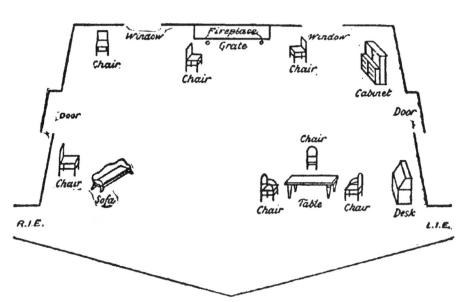

(At the rise of curtain MATHIAS *is discovered seated in armchair* R. *of table* L. DOCTOR ZIMMER *and* WILHELM *are
standing up stage in front of fireplace, regarding* MATHIAS
*intently; they go down center—*WILHELM *is leaning on the
back of table.)*

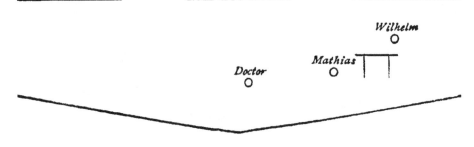

DOCTOR. You feel better, Burgomaster?

MATH. Yes, I am quite well.

DOCTOR. No more pains in the head?

MATH. No.

DOCTOR. No more strange noises in the ears?

MATH. When I tell you that I am quite well—that I never was better—that is surely enough.

WILHELM. For a long time he has had bad dreams. He talks in his sleep, and his thirst at night is constant, and feverish.

MATH. Is there anything extraordinary in being thirsty during the night?

DOCTOR. Certainly not: but you must take more care of yourself. You drink too much white wine, Burgomaster. Your attack of the night before last arose from this cause. You had taken too much wine at your cousin's, and then the severe cold having seized you, the blood had flown to the head.

MATH. I *was* cold, but that stupid gossip about the Polish Jew was the cause of all.

DOCTOR. How was that?

MATH. Well, you must know, when the Jew disappeared they brought me the cloak and cap that had belonged to the poor devil, and the sight of them quite upset me, remembering he had, the night before, stopped at our house. Since that time I had thought no more of the matter until the night before last, when some gossip brought the affair again to my mind. It was as if I had seen the ghost of the Jew. We all know that there are no such things, but—(*to* WILHELM)—Have you sent for the Notary?

WILHELM. Yes; but you must be calm.

MATH. I am calm. But Annette's marriage must take place at once. When a man in robust health and strength is liable to such an attack as I have had, nothing should be postponed till the morrow. What occurred to me the night before last might again occur to-night. I might not survive the second blow, and then I should not have seen my dear children happy. And now leave me. Whether it was the wine, or the cold, or the gossip about the Polish Jew, it comes to the same thing. It is all past and over now.

DOCTOR. But, perhaps, Burgomaster, it would be better to adjourn the signing of the marriage contract for a few days.

It is an affair of so much interest and importance that the agitation might——

MATH. (*angrily*) Good heavens, why will not people attend to their own business! I was ill, you bled me—I am well again —so much the better. Let the Notary be sent for at once. Let Father Walter and Hans be summoned as witnesses, and let the whole affair be finished without further delay.

DOCTOR. (*aside*) His nerves are still very much shaken. Perhaps it will be better to let him have his own way. (*to* MATHIAS) Well, well, we'll say no more about it. Only don't forget what I have said—be careful of the white wine.

MATH. (*angrily striking the table, turning his back*) Good! Good! Ah!

(*The* DOCTOR *looks with pity towards him, bows, and exits door,* L.—*the church bell commences to ring—Music.*)

MATH. Go and call Annette. Christian should be here by this time. Something must have detained him.

(*exit* WILHELM, *door* L.)

(*The church bells ring and the villagers in their holiday dresses pass by the window.* MATHIAS *taking a pinch of snuff from his box goes to window and salutes several who pass on. As he returns down stage to right the music stops, also the church bells.*)

All goes well! Luckily all is over. But what a lesson, Mathias,—what a lesson! Would any one believe that the mere talk about the Jew could bring on such a fit? Fortunately the people about here are such idiots they suspect nothing. (*seats himself in chair by table*) But it was that Parisian fellow at the fair who was the real cause of all. The rascal had really made me nervous. When he wanted to send me to sleep as well as the others, I said to myself, "Stop, stop, Mathias—this sending you to sleep may be an invention of the devil, you might relate certain incidents in your past life! You must be cleverer than that, Mathias; you mustn't run your neck into a halter; you must be cleverer than that—ah! you must be cleverer than that." (*starting up and crossing to* R.) You will die an old man yet, Mathias, and the most respected in the Province—(*takes snuff*) only this, since you dream and are apt to talk in your dreams, for the future you will sleep alone in the room above, the door locked, and the key safe in your pocket. They say walls have

ars—let them hear me as much as they please. (*Music—takes
unch of keys out of his pocket*) And now to count the dowry of
Annette, to be given to our dear son-in-law, in order that our
dear son-in-law may love us—(*he crosses to* L., *unlocks the
scritoire, takes out a large leather bag, unties it and empties the
contents, consisting of gold pieces and rouleaux, upon the table*)
Thirty thousand francs. (*he sits at table, front to the audience,
and commences to count the money*) Thirty thousand francs—
a fine dowry for Annette. Ah! it is pleasant to hear the sound
of gold! A fine dowry for the husband of Annette. He's a
clever fellow is Christian. He's not a Kelz—half deaf and half
blind; no, no—he's a clever fellow is Christian, and quite capable
of getting on a right track. (*a pause*) The first time I saw him
I said to myself, "You shall be my son-in-law, and if anything
should be discovered you will defend me." (*continues to count,
weighing piece upon his finger—takes up a piece and examines it*)
A piece of old gold! (*looks at it more closely—starts*) Ah! that
came from the girdle; not for them—no, no, not for them, for me.
(*places the piece of gold in his waistcoat pocket—he goes to the
scritoire, opens a drawer, takes out another piece of gold and
throws it upon the table in substitution*) That girdle did us a
good turn—without it—without it we were ruined. If Catherine
only knew—poor, poor Catherine, (*he sobs—his head sinks on his
breast—Music ceases—the Bells heard off,* L., *he starts*) The
Bells! the Bells again! They must come from the mill. (*he
rushes over to the door* R., *calls loudly:*) Franz! Franz! Franz
I say!

(*Enter* FRANZ, *door* R.; *he has an open book in his hands;
he is dressed in holiday garb—*MATHIAS *goes* C.)

       Franz   *Mathias*
       O   O

MATH. Is there any one at the mill?

FRANZ. No, Burgomaster. They have all gone to church, and the wheel is stopped.

MATH. Don't you hear the sound of Bells?

FRANZ. No, Burgomaster, I hear nothing. *(the Bells cease)*

MATH. *(aside)* Strange—strange. *(rudely)* What were you doing?

FRANZ. I was reading, Burgomaster.

MATH. Reading—what? Ghost stories, no doubt.

FRANZ. Oh, no, Burgomaster! I was reading such a curious story, about a band of robbers being discovered after twenty-three years had passed, and all through the blade of an old knife having been found in a blacksmith's shop, hidden under some rusty iron. They captured the whole of them, consisting of the mother, two sons, and the grandfather, and they hanged them all in a row. Look, Burgomaster, there's the picture. *(he shows book, which MATHIAS dashes violently from his hands)*

MATH. Enough, enough! It's pity you have nothing better to do. There, go—go! *(exit FRANZ, door R.)* *(seats himself at the table and puts remaining money into the bag)* The fools!—not to destroy all evidence against them. To be hanged through the blade of an old knife. Not like that—not like that am *I* to be caught!

> *(Music—a sprightly military air—CHRISTIAN passes at back, stops at center window and taps upon it—MATHIAS looks round, with a start, is re-assured upon seeing who it is, and says, "Ah, it is Christian!"—he ties up the bag and places it in the escritoire—CHRISTIAN enters at door, R.— MATHIAS meets him half way—they shake hands—Music ceases—CHRISTIAN is in the full dress of a Quartermaster of Gendarmes)*

CHRIS. Good morning, Burgomaster, I hope you are better.

MATH. Oh, yes, I am well, Christian. I have just been counting Annette's dowry, in good sounding gold. It was a pleasure to me to do so, as it recalled to me the days gone by, when by industry and good fortune I had been enabled to gain it; and I thought that in the future my children would enjoy and profit by all that I had so acquired.

CHRIS. You are right, Burgomaster. Money gained by honest labor is the only profitable wealth. It is the good seed which in time is sure to bring a rich harvest.

MATH. Yes, yes; especially when the good seed is sown in good ground. The contract must be signed to-day.

CHRIS. To-day?

MATH. Yes, the sooner the better. I hate postponements. Once decided, why adjourn the business? It shows a great want of character.

CHRIS. Well, Burgomaster, nothing to me could be more agreeable.

MATH. Annette loves you.

CHRIS. Ah, she does.

MATH. And the dowry is ready—then why should not the affair be settled at once? I hope, my boy, you will be satisfied.

CHRIS. You know, Burgomaster, I do not bring much.

MATH. You bring courage and good conduct—I will take care of the rest; and now let us talk of other matters. You are late to-day. I suppose you were busy. Annette waited for you, and was obliged to go without you.

(MATHIAS *goes up center and seats himself in chair by the fire; he takes up the tongs and arranges the fire.*)

(CHRISTIAN *lays his hat on the table* L.; *he unbuckles his sword and lays that also on table, then seats himself on chair on the opposite side from* MATHIAS *at fireplace.*)

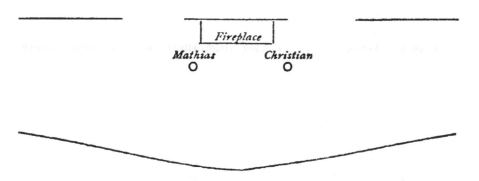

CHRIS. Ah, it was very curious business that detained me. Would you believe it, Burgomaster, I was reading old depositions from five o'clock till ten? The hours flew by, but the more I read, the more I wished to read.

MATH. And what was the subject of the depositions?

CHRIS. They were about the case of the Polish Jew who was murdered on the Bridge of Vechem fifteen years ago.

MATH. (*dropping the tongs*) Ah!

CHRIS. Father Walter told me the story the night before last. It seems to me very remarkable that nothing was ever discovered.

MATH. No doubt—no doubt.

CHRIS. The man who committed that murder must have been a clever fellow.

MATH. Yes, he was not a fool.

CHRIS. A fool! He would have made one of the cleverest gendarmes in the department.

MATH. (*with a smile*) Do you really think so?

CHRIS. I am sure of it. There are so many ways of detecting criminals, and so few escape, that to have committed a crime like this, and yet to remain undiscovered, showed the possession of extraordinary address.

MATH. I quite agree with you, Christian; and what you say shows your good sense. When a man has committed a crime, and by it gained money, he becomes like a gambler, and tries his second and his third throw. I should think it requires a great amount of courage to resist the first success in crime.

CHRIS. You are right, but what is most remarkable to me in the case is this, that no trace of the murdered man was ever found. Now do you know what my idea is?

MATH. (*rising*) No, no! What is your idea? (*they come forward*)

CHRIS. Well, I find at that time there were a great many lime-kilns in the neighborhood of Vechem. Now it is my idea that the murderer, to destroy all traces of his crime, threw the body of the Jew into one of these kilns. Old Kelz, my predecessor, evidently never thought of that.

MATH. Very likely—very likely. Do you know that idea never occurred to me. You are the first who ever suggested it.

CHRIS. And this idea led me to many others. Now suppose—suppose inquiry had been instituted as to those persons who were burning lime at that time.

MATH. Take care, Christian—take care. Why, I, myself, had a lime-kiln burning at the time the crime was committed.

CHRIS. (*laughing*) Oh, you, Burgomaster? (*he goes up stage and looks out of window*)

(MATHIAS *remains down stage; enter* WILHELM *through door* L.)

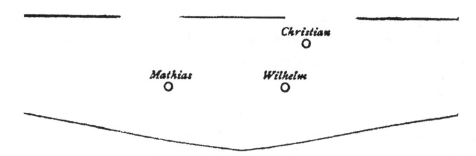

MATH. Is the Notary here yet?

WILHELM. Yes, (*pointing to door* L.) he is in the next room rith Father Walter and Hans, and the others. He is reading the ontract to them now.

MATH. Good, good—(*he goes up stage and calls off* L.) Now ο sign the contract. Walter, Hans, come in! Let every man ome in! The most important acts in life should always take lace in the presence of all men. It is an old and honest custom ι Alsace.

(**Lively music until all are in position.*)

(*Enter through door* L., HANS, WALTER, ten PEASANTS *and the* NOTARY. *The peasantry wear ribbons in their buttonholes and keep their hats on. They group about the stage.* MATHIAS *shakes hands with everybody and conducts the* NOTARY *to the left of the table.*)

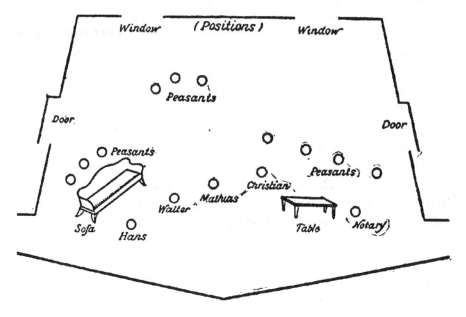

NOTARY. Gentlemen and witnesses,—You have just heard read the marriage contract between Christian Bême, Quartermaster of Gendarmes, and Annette Mathias. Has anyone any observations to make?

SEVERAL VOICES. No, no.

NOTARY. Then we can at once proceed to take the signatures. (MATHIAS *goes to the escritoire and takes out the bag of gold which he places on the table before the* NOTARY) There is the dowry. It is not in promises made on paper, but in gold. Thirty thousand francs in good French gold.

ALL. Thirty thousand francs!

CHRISTIAN. It is too much, Burgomaster.

MATH. Not at all, not at all. When Catherine and myself are gone there will be more. And now, Christian, (*Music commences*) I wish you to make me one promise.

CHRIS. What promise?

(MATHIAS *stands* R. C.—CHRISTIAN L. C.)

MATH. Young men are ambitious. It is natural they should be. You must promise me that you will remain in this village while both of us live. You know Annette is our only child; we love her dearly, and to lose her altogether would break our hearts. Do you promise?

CHRIS. I do promise.

MATH. Your word of honor given before all?

CHRIS. My word of honor given before all. (*they shake hands*)
(**Music stops.*)

MATH. (*crossing to* L. *corner, and taking pinch of snuff— aside*) It was necessary. And now to sign the contract. (*he goes to table; the* NOTARY *hands him the pen, and points to the place where he is to sign his name*—MATHIAS *is about to write—the Bells heard off*—MATHIAS *stops, listens with terror —his face to the audience, and away from the persons upon the stage—aside*) Bells! Courage, Mathias! (*after an effort he signs rapidly—the Bells cease—he throws the pen down*) Come, Christian, sign! (CHRISTIAN *approaches the table to sign—as he is about to do so* WALTER *taps him on the shoulder*—MATHIAS *starts at the interruption.*)

WALTER. It is not every day you sign a contract like that.

(ALL *laugh*—MATHIAS *heaves a sigh and is re-assured—*
    CHRISTIAN *signs—*

MATH. Now see Annette and Catherine and let them sign. CHRISTIAN *runs off* L. *door*)

(MATHIAS *seats himself in chair* R. *of table. The characters and peasants sing a chorus as the curtain descends slowly.*)

END OF ACT II.

ACT III.

A bedroom in the Burgomaster's house. A gauze drop in 2, painted to represent the side of a chamber; this is immediately backed by another drop. There is a door to lock R. 2 E. and an alcove L., which contains a bed. The alcove is covered with plain curtains. There is a table on the up side of the alcove and a chair at the lower end. Back of the drops in 2 there is another set representing a courtroom. An interior drop in 5. Sides may be boxed or the entrances open—A large desk center on a platform. A partition on either side of stage about three feet high to enclose the public. When this back set is used the stage calcium is thrown freely upon it, whilst the house lights, the foot and front border lights are low.—Time, night. *Music at rise—stage lights up when the characters enter at rise.

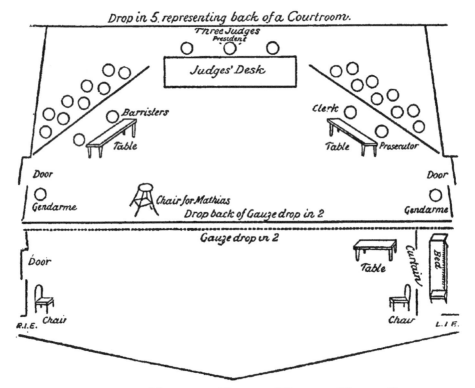

(*Enter door* R.—MATHIAS, FATHER WALTER, HANS, CHRISTIAN, WILHELM. FRANZ *carries a lighted candle, a bottle of water and a glass, which he places on table by the alcove. The men appear to feel their wine.*)

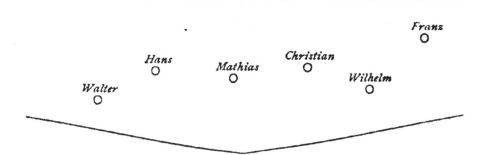

HANS. (*laughing*) Ha! ha! everything has gone off admirably. We only wanted something to wind up with, and I may say that we are all as capitally wound up as the great clock at Strasbourg. (FRANZ *goes off through door* R.)

WALTER. Yes, and what wine we have consumed? For many a day we shall remember the signing of Annette's marriage contract. I shall like to witness such a contract every second day.

HANS. There, I object to your argument. Every day, I say!

CHRIS. (*to* MATHIAS) And so you are determined, Mathias, to sleep here to-night.

MATH. Yes, I am decided. I wish for air. I know what is necessary for my condition. The heat was the cause of my accident. This room is cooler, and will prevent its recurrence. (*laughter heard outside*)

HANS. Listen, how they are still revelling! Come, Father Walter, let us rejoin the revels!

WALTER. But Mathias already deserts us, just at the moment when we were beginning to thoroughly enjoy ourselves.

MATH. What more do you wish me to do? From noon till midnight is surely enough!

WALTER. Enough, it may be, but not too much; never too much of such wine.

HANS. There, again, I object to your argument—never enough, I say.

WILHELM. Mathias is right. You remember that Doctor Zimmer told him to be careful of the wine he took, or it would one day play him false. He has already taken too much since this morning.

MATH. One glass of water before I go to rest is all I require. It will calm me—it will calm me.

(KARL, FRITZ *and* TONY, *three of the guests of the previous act, enter suddenly, slightly merry, pushing each other.*)

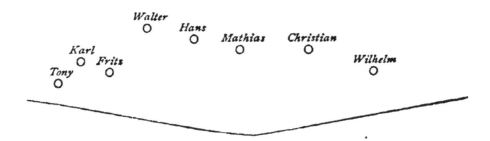

GUESTS. Good night, Burgomaster. Good night.

TONY. I say, Hans! don't you know that the Night Watchman is below?

HANS. The Night Watchman! What in the name of all that is polite, does he want?

KARL. He requires us all to leave, and the house to be closed. It is past hours.

MATH. Give him a bumper of wine, and then good night all!

WALTER. Past hours! For a Burgomaster no regulations ought to exist.

HANS. ⎫
OTHERS. ⎬ Certainly not.

MATH. (*with fierceness*) Regulations made for all must be obeyed by all.

WALTER. (*timidly*) Well, then, shall we go?

MATH. Yes, yes, go! Leave me to myself.

WALTER. (*shaking hands with* MATHIAS) *Good night,* Mathias. I wish you calm repose, and no unpleasant dreams.

MATH. (*fiercely*) I never dream. (*mildly*) Good night, all. Go, friends, go.

(WALTER, HANS *and guests exeunt door* R.—WILHELM *and* CHRISTIAN *remain.*)

MATH. Good night, brother. (*shakes hands with* WILHELM) I shall be better here. The wine, the riot and those songs have quite dazed my brain. I shall sleep better here, I shall sleep better.

CHRIS. The room is fresh and cool. Good night.

MATH. The same to you Christian, the same to you. (*they hake hands*) Good night; do not fear for me; good night.

(CHRISTIAN *and* WILHELM, *exeunt door* R.)

Music ceases—he goes up cautiously, locks the door, R., and puts the key in his pocket.)

At last I am alone! Everything goes well. Christian the endarme is caught! To-night I shall sleep without a fear aunting me! If any new danger should threaten the father-in-aw of the Quartermaster, it would soon be averted. Ah! What power it is to know how to guide your destiny in life. You iust hold good cards in your hands. Good cards! as I have one, and if you play them well you may defy ill fortune.

Chorus of REVELLERS, *outside* (*without accompaniment*).

Now, since we must part, let's drain a last glass;
        Let's drink!
Let us first drink to this gentle young lass;
        Let's drink!
From drinking this toast, we'll none of us shrink;
Others shall follow, when we've time to think.
    Our burden shall be, let us drink!
    The burden to bear is good drink.

                    (*loud laughter heard outside*)

MATH. (*taking off his coat*) Ha, ha, ha! Those jolly topers ave got all they want. What holes in the snow they will make efore they reach their homes! Drink! Drink! Is it not strange? `o drink and drown every remorse! Yes, everything goes well! *he drinks a glass of water*) Mathias, you can at least boast f having well managed your affairs—the contract signed—rich— rosperous—respected—happy! (*takes off waistcoat*) No one now ill hear you, if you dream. No one! No more folly!—no more ells! To-night, I triumph; for conscience is at rest!

(*he enters the alcove—the Chorus of Revellers heard again, in the distance—a hand is extended from alcove and extinguishes the candle—stage dark—curtain at back of gauze rises, disclosing an extensive set of a Court of Justice, arched, brilliantly lighted—at back, three* JUDGES *on the bench, dressed in black caps and red robes—at* R. *and* L., *the* PUBLIC, *in Alsatian costumes—in front of the* JUDGES, *but beneath them, a table, on which lies the Jew's cloak and cap —on* R., *the* PUBLIC PROSECUTOR *and* BARRISTERS—*on* L., *the*

CLERK *or* REGISTRAR OF THE COURT, *and* BARRISTERS—*a* GEN-DARME *at each corner of the Court*—MATHIAS *is discovered seated on a stool in* C. *of Court—he is dressed in the brown blouse and hood worn by the* MAN *in the vision in Act I.—he has his back to the* AUDIENCE, *face to* JUDGES)

THE CLERK OF THE COURT. (L., *standing, reading the Act of Accusation*)   Therefore, the prisoner, Mathias, is accused of having, on the night of the 24th December, 1818, between midnight and one o'clock, assassinated the Jew Kovesky, upon the bridge of Vechem, to rob him of his gold.

PRESIDENT.   Prisoner, you have heard the Act of Accusation read; you have already heard the depositions of the witnesses. What have you to say in answer?

MATH.   (*violently—throws back hood, and starting up*) Witnesses! People who saw nothing; people who live miles from the place where the crime was committed; at night, and in the winter time! You call such people witnesses!

PRES.   Answer with calmness; these gestures—this violence will avail you nothing. You are a man full of cunning.

MATH.   (*with humility*) No, I am a man of simplicity.

PRES.   You knew well the time to select; you knew well how to evade all suspicion; you knew well how to destroy all direct evidence. You are a dangerous man!

MATH.   (*derisively*) Because nothing can be proved against me I am dangerous! Every honest man then is dangerous when nothing can be proved against him! A rare encouragement for honesty!

PRES.   The public voice accuses you. Answer me this: How is it that you hear the noise of Bells?

MATH.   (*passionately*) I do not hear the noise of Bells! (*music—Bells heard off as before—*MATHIAS *trembles*)

PRES.   Prisoner, you speak falsely. At this moment you hear that noise. Tell us why is this?

MATH.   It is nothing. It is simply a jangling in my ears.

PRES.   Unless you acknowledge the true cause of this noise you hear, we shall summon the Mesmerist to explain the matter to us.

MATH.   (*with defiance*) It is true then that I hear this noise. (*Bells cease*)

PRES. (*to the* CLERK *of the* COURT) It is well, write that down.

MATH. Yes; but I hear it in a dream.

PRES. Write, that he hears it in a dream.

MATH. (*furiously*) Is it a crime to dream?

THE CROWD. (*murmur very softly among themselves, and move simultaneously, each person performing exactly the same movement of negation*) N—N—N—o!

(MATHIAS *rises from his seat and addresses himself to the public on either side of stage.*)

MATH. (*with confidence*) Listen, friends! Don't fear for me! All this is but a dream—I am in a dream. If it were not a dream should I be clothed in these rags? Should I have before me such judges as these? Judges who, simply acting upon their own empty ideas, would hang a fellow creature. Ha, ha, ha! It is a dream—a dream! (*he bursts into a long derisive laugh*)

(MATHIAS *sits and faces audience.*)

PRES. Silence, prisoner—silence! (*turning to his companion judges*) Gentlemen—this noise of Bells arises in the prisoner's mind from the remembrance of what is past. The prisoner hears this noise because there rankles in his heart the memory of that he would conceal from us. The Jew's horse carried Bells.

MATH. It is false, I have no memories.

PRES. Be silent!

MATH. (*with rage*) A man cannot be condemned upon such suppositions. You must have proofs. I do not hear the noise of Bells.

PRES. You see, gentlemen, the prisoner contradicts himself. He has already made the avowal—now he retracts it.

MATH. No! I hear nothing. (*the Bells heard*) It is the blood rushing to my brain—this jangling in my ears. (*the Bells increase in sound*) I ask for Christian. Why is not Christian here? (*he turns from side to side and speaks nervously*)

PRES. Prisoner! do you persist in your denial?

MATH. (*with force*) Yes. There is nothing proved against me. It is a gross injustice to keep an honest man in prison. I suffer in the cause of justice. (*the Bells cease*)

PRES. You persist. Well! Considering that since this affair took place fifteen years have passed, and that it is impossible to throw light upon the circumstances by ordinary means—first, through the cunning and audacity of the prisoner, and second, through the deaths of witnesses who could have given evidence —for these reasons we decree that the Court hear the Mesmerist. Officer, summon the Mesmerist.

MATH. (*in a terrible voice*) I oppose it! I oppose it! Dreams prove nothing.

PRES. Summon the Mesmerist!   (*exit* GENDARME, R.)

MATH. (*striking the table*) It is abominable! It is in defiance of all justice!

(MATHIAS *is standing back of his chair,* L. *of table* R.)

PRES. If you are innocent, why should you fear the Mesmerist, because he can read the inmost secrets of your heart? Be calm, or, believe me, your own indiscretion will prove that you are guilty.

MATH. I demand an advocate. I wish to instruct the advocate Linder of Saverne. In a case like this, I do not care for cost. I am calm—as calm as any man who has no reproach against himself. I fear nothing; but dreams are dreams. (*loudly*) Why is Christian not here? My honor is his honor! Let him be sent for. He is an honest man. (*with exultation*) Christian, I have made you rich. Come, and defend me!

(MATHIAS *seats himself again. During all his movements one of the calcium lights follow him during this scene.*)

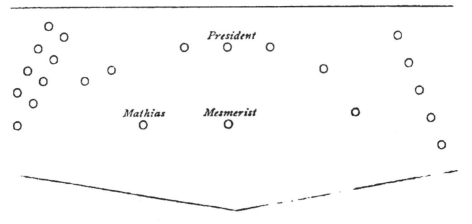

Music—the GENDARME *who had gone out, returns with the* MESMERIST.

MESMER. (*bending to the Court respectfully*) Your honors, the President and Judges of the Court, it is your decree that has brought me before your tribunal; without such direction, terror alone would have kept me far from here.

(MATHIAS *rises and turns toward the* PRESIDENT.)

MATH. Who can believe in the follies of the Mesmerists? They deceive the public for the purpose of gaining money! They merely perform the tricks of conjurors! I have seen this fellow already at my cousin Bôth's, at Ribeauville.

PRES. (*to the* MESMERIST) Can you send this man to sleep?

MESMER. (*looking full at* MATHIAS, *who sinks upon chair, unable to endure the* MESMERIST'S *gaze*) I can!

MATH. (*starting up*) I will not be made the subject of this conjuror's experiments.

PRES. I command it!

MATH. Christian—where is Christian? He will prove that I am an honest man.

PRES. Your resistance betrays you.

MATH. (*with defiance*) I have no fear. (*sits*)

(*The* MESMERIST *makes several passes—waving his out-stretched hands—in front and back of* MATHIAS, *his eyes being intently fixed upon him. This is kept up for about ten seconds. *Music tremulo.*)

MATH. (*to himself*) Mathias, if you sleep you are lost. (*his eyes are fixed as if struck with horror—in a hollow voice*) No—no—I will not sleep—I—will—(*in a hesitating voice*) I will—not —no——(*falls asleep—Music ceases*)

MESMER. (*to the* PRESIDENT) He sleeps. What shall I ask him?

PRES. Ask him, what he did on the night of the 24th of December, fifteen years ago.

MESMER. (*to* MATHIAS, *in a firm voice*) You are at the night of the 24th December, 1818?

MATH. (*in a low voice*) Yes.

MESMER. What time is it?

MATH. Half-past eleven.

MESMER. Speak on, I command you!

MATH. (*still in the same attitude, speaking as if he were describing a vision presented to his sight*) The people are leaving the inn—Catherine and Little Annette have gone to rest. Our man Kasper comes in. He tells me the lime-kiln is lighted. I answer him, it is well; go to bed, I will see to the kiln. He leaves me; I am alone with the Jew, who warms himself at the stove. Outside, everything sleeps. Nothing is heard, except from time to time the Jew's horse under the shed, when he shakes his bells.

MESMER. Of what are you thinking?

MATH. I am thinking that I must have money—that if I have not three thousand francs by the 31st, the inn will be taken from me. I am thinking that no one is stirring; that it is night; that there are two feet of snow upon the ground, and that the Jew will follow the high road quite alone!

MESMER. Have you already decided to attack him?

MATH. (*after a short silence*) That man is strong. He has broad shoulders. I am thinking that he would defend himself well, should anyone attack him. (*he makes a movement*)

MESMER. What ails you?

MATH. (*in a low voice*) He looks at me. He has gray eyes. (*as if speaking to himself*) I must strike the blow!

MESMER. You are decided?

MATH. Yes—yes; I will strike the blow! I will risk it!

MESMER. Go on!

MATH. (*continuing*) I must, however, look round. I go out; all is dark! It still snows; no one will trace my footsteps in the snow. (*he raises his hand as if feeling for something*)

MESMER. What are you doing?

MATH. I am feeling in the sledge—should he carry pistols! There is nothing—I will strike the blow! (*he listens*) All is silent in the village! Little Annette is crying; a goat bleats in the stable; the Jew is walking in his room!

MESMER. You re-enter?

MATH. Yes. The Jew has placed six francs upon the table; I return him his money; he fixes his eyes steadily upon me!

(MATHIAS *takes plenty of time describing the occurrence.*)

MESMER. He speaks to you?

MATH. He asks me how far it is to Mutzig? Four leagues. I wish him well on his journey! He answers—"God bless you!" He goes out—He is gone! (MATHIAS, *with body bent, takes several steps forward as if following and watching his victim, he extends his hands*) The axe! Where is the axe? Ah, here, behind the door! How cold it is! (*he trembles*) The snow falls

—not a star! Courage, Mathias, you shall possess the girdle—courage!

MESMER. You follow him?

MATH. Yes, yes. I have crossed the fields! (*pointing*) Here is the old bridge, and there below, the frozen rivulet! How the dogs howl at Daniel's farm—how they howl! And old Finck's forge, how brightly it glows upon the hillock. (*low, as if speaking to himself*) Kill a man!—kill a man! You will not do that, Mathias—you will not do that! Heaven forbids it. (*proceeding to walk with measured steps and bent body*) You are a fool! Listen, you will be rich, your wife and child will no longer want for anything! The Jew came; so much the worse—so much the worse. He ought not to have come! You will pay all you owe; you will no more be in debt. (*loud, in a broken tone*) It must be, Mathias, that you kill him! (*he listens*) No one on the road—no one! (*with an expression of terror*) What dreadful silence! (*he wipes his forehead with his hand*) One o'clock strikes, and the moon shines. Ah! The Jew has already passed! Thank God! thank God! (*he kneels—a pause—he listens—the Bells heard without as before*) No! The Bells! The Bells! He comes! (*he bends down in a watching attitude, and remains still—a pause—in a low voice*) You will be rich—you will be rich—you will be rich! (*the noise of the Bells increase—the* CROWD *express alarm simultaneously—all at once* MATHIAS *springs forward, and with a species of savage roar, strikes a terrible blow with his right hand*) Ah! ah! I have you now, Jew! (*he strikes again—the* CROWD *simultaneously express horror—* MATHIAS *leans forward and gazes anxiously on the ground—he extends his hand as if to touch something, but draws it back in horror*) He does not move! (*he raises himself, utters a deep sigh of relief and looks round*) The horse has fled with the sledge! (*the Bells cease—kneeling down*) Quick, quick! The girdle! I have it. Ha! (*he performs the action in saying this of taking it from the Jew's body and buckling it round his own*) It is full of gold, quite full. Be quick, Mathias, be quick! Carry him away. (*he bends low down and appears to lift the body upon his back; then he walks across stage, his body bent, his step slow as a man who carries a heavy load*)

MESMER. Where are you going?

MATH. (*stopping*) To the lime-kiln. I am there. (*he appears *to throw the body upon the kiln)* How heavy he was! *(he breathes with force, then he again bends down to take up a pole—in a hoarse voice)* Go into the fire, Jew, go into the fire! *(he appears to push the body with the pole using his whole force, suddenly he utters a cry of horror and staggers away, his face covered with his hands)* Those eyes, oh, those eyes! How he glares at me. *(he sinks on to stool, and takes the same attitude as when first thrown into sleep).*

PRES. *(with a sign to the* MESMERIST*)* It is well. *(to the* CLERK OF THE COURT*)* You have written all?

CLERK. All!

PRES. *(to* MESMERIST*)* It is well—awake him now, and let him read himself.

MESMER. Awake! I command you!

MATH. *(awakes gradually—he appears bewildered)* Where am I? *(he looks round)* Ah! Yes; what is going on?

CLERK. *(goes over to him and hands him a paper)* Here is your deposition—read it.

*(*MATHIAS *rises and partially faces the* JUDGES*.)*

MATH. *(takes it and, before reading it, aside)* Wretched, wretched fool! I have told all; I am lost! *(with rage, after reading the paper)* It is false! *(tears the paper into pieces)* You are a set of rogues! Christian—where is Christian? It is a crime against justice! They will not let my only witness speak. Christian! They would kill the father of your wife! Help me—help me!

PRES. You force me to speak of an event of which I had wished to remain silent. Your son-in-law Christian, upon hearing of the crimes with which you are charged, by his own hand sought his death. He is no more.

MATH. Ah! *(he appears stupefied with dismay)*

PRES. *(after consulting the other* JUDGES*, rises, speaks in a solemn tone of voice)* Considering that on the night of the 24th December, 1818, between midnight and one o'clock, Mathias committed the crime of assassination upon the person of one Koveski, and considering that this crime was committed under circumstances which aggravates its enormity—such as premeditation, and for the purpose of highway robbery; the Court condemns the said Mathias to be hanged by the neck until he is dead!

(MATHIAS *staggers and falls on his knees—the* CROWD *make a movement of terror—the death-bell tolls—lights lowered gradually—then curtain at back of gauze descends, disclosing the scene as at commencement—lights up—*Lively music—a peal of joy bells heard ringing*)

CROWD. (*outside shouting*) Christian, Annette. (*loud knocking at door,* R.)

WILHELM. (*without*) Mathias! Mathias! brother! get up at once. It is late in the morning and all our guests are below. (*knocking on door,* R.)

CHRIS. (*without*) Mathias! Mathias! (*silence*) How soundly he sleeps!

WALTER. (*without*) Ho! Mathias, the wedding has commenced. (*more knocking*)

THE CROWD. (*aside*) Burgomaster! Burgomaster! (*loud knocking*)

WILHELM. (*in an anxious voice*) He does not answer. It is strange. Mathias! (*a discussion among many voices is heard without*)

CHRIS. No—It is useless. Leave it to me! (*at the same moment several violent blows are struck upon the door, which falls into the room from its hinges*)

(*Enter* CHRISTIAN, *hurriedly—he runs to the alcove—Music, hurry.*)

CHRIS. Mathias! (*looks into alcove and staggers back into room*) Ah!

(*Enter from door* R., HANS, WALTER, WILHELM, FRANZ, DOCTOR ZIMMER *and all the* GUESTS, *dressed for the wedding.*)

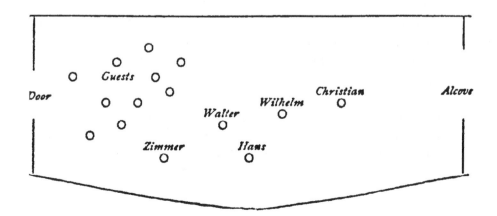

WILHELM. What has happened, Christian, what has happened?
(*advancing toward alcove*)

CHRIS. (*stopping him*) Don't come near—don't come near.

WILHELM. (*striving to pass*) I will see what it is. Let me
pass. I will see my brother.

(MATHIAS *appears from the alcove—he is dressed in the
same clothes as when he retired into the alcove at the
commencement of the Scene, but his face is haggard, and
ghastly pale—he comes out, his eyes fixed, his arms extended—as he rushes forward with uncertain steps, the
CROWD fall back with horror, and form groups of con-
sternation, with a general exclamation of terror*)

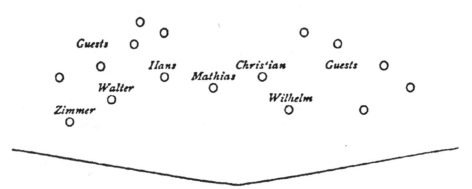

MATH.   (*in a voice of strangulation*) The rope! the rope!
Cut the rope!

(*he falls suddenly, and is caught in the arms of* HANS *and*
WALTER, *who carry him to the chair in center of stage—
the Bells heard off—Music, the melody played in the
Second Act when promise given—his hands clutch at his
throat as if to remove something that strangles him—he
looks pitifully round as if trying to recognize those about
him, and then his head falls on his breast—*

CHRIS. (*kneels and places his hand over* MATHIAS' *heart*)
Dead! Dead! (*the Bells stop*) *Music continues until curtain.
CHRISTIAN *and* WILHELM *kneel and bow their heads. All the
characters remove their hats. General dejection.*)

SLOW CURTAIN.

THE END.

God-Speed

FOR ALL OCCASIONS.

With an Appendix of Prose Compositions,
Salutatory Addresses and Valedictory Orations for School Festivals.

PRICE, Bound in Cloth, - - - - - - 75 Cents.

TABLE OF CONTENTS.

e above description, and contents and specimens of GOD-SPEED found on next
at usefulness and opportuneness of this entirely new and original book will be

u this book has been especially composed and written for it by competent
and, while exaggerated and bombastic style has been scrupulously avoided,
to render the pieces, in thought and expression, worthy of the name Poetry.

acter and scope has not existed, in our language, previous to this.

supplies appropriate sentiment, clothed in beautiful language, for
in human life, and there is hardly anybody to whom the book
iceable on many occasions.

nal Institutions this book is altogether indispensable. The
ADDRESSES and VALEDICTORY ORATIONS for School
l service.

BARCLAY STREET, NEW YORK

This Book has just been adopted as Tex‍
ST. FRANCIS XAVIER'S COLLEGE,

Select Recitations, Orations and Dramatic Scenes

with Actions and Emphasis

AN ELOCUTIONARY MANUAL

Containing 100 Selections from the Leading Poets, Orators and Dramatists, supplied with copious and minute directions for their CORRECT, GRACEFUL and IMPRESSIVE DELIVERY.

By C. J. BIRBECK
Professor of Elocution and English Literature

PRICE, bound in cloth, $1.00

This volume, which contains the Movements and Gestures suitable to the recitations, the Emphatic Words properly marked, and directions relative Time, Pitch, and Force in marginal notes, will be found very useful not o to the Student but also to the Class Teacher. The selections found i book are strictly moral in tone, choice in literary merits, evenly divers‍ sentiment and graded to the capabilities of all students.

From a number of flattering testimonials, the following one ‍
The REV. J. H. McGEAN, P.R., St. Peter's Church, Ne‍
adopting this volume for the elocution class of his school, w‍
"*The selections, both dramatic and oratorical, will con‍ students of elocution, and will be welcomed by all who cul‍ rect speaking and reading by their pupils. The full d‍ gesture (a new feature in such a work) will aid both t‍*
A copy of the book is mailed free upon receipt o‍
Correspondence with a view to introduction i‍ the publisher.

JOSEPH F. WAGNER, 9 BARCLAY‍

Hollinger Corp.
pH 8.5

CPSIA information can be obtained at www.ICGtesting.com
Printed in the USA
LVOW02s1832190114

370040LV00021B/337/P